# Ancient Chapels
# and Churches in Wales

Published and printed in Wales
by Y Lolfa Cyf., Talybont, Ceredigion SY24 5AP
*e-mail* ylolfa@ylolfa.com
*website* www.ylolfa.com
*tel.* (01970) 832 304
*fax* 832 782
*isdn* 832 813

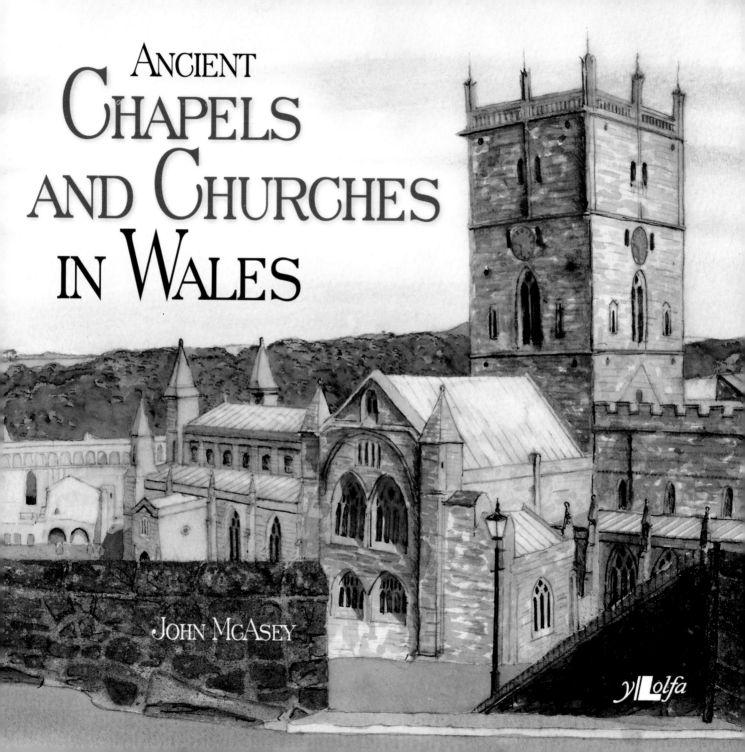

# Ancient Chapels and Churches in Wales

John McAsey

Y Lolfa

St Patrick's Church

Capel Lligwy

St Cybi's Church

Penmon Priory

St Tudno's Church

St Trillo's Chapel

St Winefride's Well & Chapel

St Cwyfan's Church

St Tysilio's Church

St Beuno's Church

The Hospice Church

St Hywyn's Church

St Tanwg's Church

St Melangell's Church

St Mary's Abbey

St Celynin's Church

St Padarn's Church

St Mary Magdalen Church

St Dogmael's Abbey

St Brynach's Church
Cwm yr Eglwys

St Brynach's Church Nevern

St Gwyndaf's Church

St. Justinian's Chapel

St. Hywel's Church

St. David's

St. Non's Chapel

St Govan's Chapel

Caldey Island Monastery

Margam Abbey

Tin Ab

Llandaf Cathedral

St Illtyd's Church

# Contents

# Introduction

The following pages are an appreciation and visual documentary of Celtic chapels and ancient churches in Wales. Although I thought that I knew every area of this country – from coast to mountain, from isolated village to the capital city of Wales, I discovered places that I had never been to before.

A large amount of my research has involved the study of people, places and events originating in the 5th–8th centuries. This was when the Romans had left Britain; a period of history known as the Dark Ages, a time steeped in myths and legends. King Arthur ruled, and the Druids still had great influence over the Celtic people.

This time was also known as the Age of Saints, which refers to the wandering monks and holy men who Christianised Wales. These Celtic saints were different to those of the Roman church, because at this time, anyone who dedicated themselves to the religious life were known as 'saints'.

Throughout Wales, villages and towns are named after these Welsh saints, such as Llanbadrig, after St Patrick or Llandudno, after St Tudno. In other cases, parts of the landscape may refer to a long-forgotten saint, such as St Govans Head or St Justinians Bay.

Other natural features were also named in this way, for example wells or springs, with St Winifride's well being the most famous, others include St Beuno's well, where the waters may have curative powers.

There are scores of legends associated with many of these saints, the most notable of which are their association with King Arthur, whom some historians claim had his court in Wales at this period. I have included some of these myths and fables associated with the saints, buildings or locations. I have followed the ancient pilgrims' routes, along the Llŷn Road to Bardsey Island, through Clynnog Fawr, Nefyn and Tudweiliog, in search of Celtic foundations. In the days of the pilgrims, there would have been many resting places along the route – each with accommodation, priest and holy well, such as the ancient Hospice church at Pistyll – before finally arriving at the pilgrims' church at Aberdaron. The other main pilgrim routes that I followed were the coastal roads leading to St David's, with many interesting chapels and churches along the way.

I have also visited the islands around Wales, where some early Celtic saints lived – notably Bardsey, where the monks sought solitude, undertaking harsh lives of prayer, contemplation and manual labour. A number of saints established chapels on other islands; St Tysilio on Church Island on the Menai Straits and St Samson on Caldey Island, for example.

In this book I have endeavoured to present the majority of Celtic chapels in Wales which are still standing, plus many of the more important churches and abbeys whose foundations go back over 1,000 years. Hopefully I have selected those which are the most interesting with regard to their architecture, folklore or location; many are sited in spectacular landscapes, such as St Non's chapel or Penmon Priory. Others may lack visual interest, but have been included because of their important history. St Padarn's church in Llanbadarn Fawr – which in the middle ages was one of the major cultural centres in Wales – is one such church.

In conclusion, the chapels and churches have been chosen not only because they are some of the oldest buildings in Britain, but also for the story they tell in the history of our country and their place within the sacred landscape of Wales.

**John McAsey**
**2003**

# St Tudno's Church – Llandudno, Gwynedd

St Tudno's church is situated on a dramatic spot on the Great Orme overlooking the sea above Llandudno.

St Tudno was said to be one of the seven sons of Seithenyn, a ruler of the kingdom of Cantref y Gwaelod, which, according to legend, lies beneath the sea in Cardigan Bay when the sea flooded the land. Tudno and his brothers managed to escape the flood and went to the monastery of Bangor-is-y-Coed, where he studied and became a monk.

His missionary journeys were extensive and he eventually arrived at the Great Orme, where he established his first cell on the shore at Ogof Llech, in a small limestone cave with a spring. St Tudno then built his first church on the headland above his cell; he may have chosen this spot because it was the location of an earlier pagan site of worship, or because of the two wells nearby – the Roman well and St Tudno's well.

The original building was a square construction, made of wood, with a thatched roof. In the 12th century, the church was rebuilt in stone, and the size increased to that of the present nave. In the late 15th century, the small church was widened and a chancel was built.

Over the years the church was neglected, and in January 1839 a severe storm badly damaged the roof and the building. It became dilapidated and was left to decay.

However, in 1855 the sum of £100 was raised to re-roof the building, and later a benefactor undertook to completely renovate the church. During the renovation a number of ancient frescos were discovered; unfortunately these have not survived.

Inside the church there are a number of interesting features such as the carved round font dating back to the 12th century, which was lost for many years before being recovered from a local farm, where it was used as an animal trough. Other features include painted panels of the Creed, the Lord's Prayer, and the Ten Commandments in Welsh.

One legend associated with the church is that it housed one of the thirteen ancient treasures of Britain; this was St Tudno's whetstone, which sharpened the swords of heroes, but blunted those of cowards.

# St Padarn's Church –

## Llanbadarn Fawr, Ceredigion

The church of St Padarn is situated in the village of Llanbadarn Fawr in the Rheidol Valley, near Aberystwyth.

St Padarn who was one of a number of Celtic missionaries who came to Wales from Brittany and founded a monastery here in the 6th century. There is one story concerning Padarn which relates that King Maelgwn sent two servants with bags of treasure to Llanbadarn Fawr for safekeeping. Later the servants returned to collect the bags for Maelgwn, but the King found only stones in them and accused Padarn of theft, so along with the servants, Padarn agreed to submit to a trial by boiling water. All three submerged their hands but only the servants were scalded, proving that Padarn was innocent. As an apology Maelgwn gave him lands to build his monastery between the rivers of Rheidol and Clarach, where he was bishop and abbot for 20 years. This monastery was typical of those found in Celtic Britain and although it was ransacked by the Saxons in 720 AD, by the 11th century it had grown considerably, becoming one of the main cultural centres of Wales. The library here was said to be larger than those of Canterbury Cathedral and York Minster. Parts of the existing church dates from about 1257, replacing the earlier church which had been destroyed by fire. However the majority of the present building dates from the 15th century, including the chancel with large windows on three sides. It is cruciform in shape, with a large central tower, the size reflects the importance of this church – the mother church of what was at that time the largest parish in Wales. Other features of interest include two Celtic stone crosses which stand in the south transept; one, 10 feet high, is intricately carved, dating from about 750 AD and is one of the finest in Wales, the other 5ft high, probably dates from the time of the original monastery. For centuries, the crosses stood in the churchyard; however they were brought to their present position in 1916.

# St Tysilio's Church –

## Llandysilo Island, Menai Bridge, Anglesey

The church is in an idylic setting on an island in the Menai Straits below the Menai Bridge which can only be reached by walking along a causeway. The church was originally established in the 7th Century by St Tysilio who was a Prince of Powys and the son of King Brochwel of Powys. The King had decided that Tysilio should become a knight but he was committed to the religious life, so he fled from his father's influence and went to a monastery in Meifod, Powys to train to be a monk. From there, he came to this island to live, this was to become a centre for his missionary work on Anglesey. Celtic monks sought out islands as they were thought to be holy places, where they could live the life of a hermit in prayer and contemplation.

After seven years on the island, Tysilio returned to Meifod and became an abbot, after which he went to Brittany to establish a monastery at St Malo, where he died. Islands such as this were considered holy places by the early Christians; they were ideal places for the solitary, contemplative life of prayer and meditation that the Celtic monks sought.

The present church was built in the early 14th century on the foundations of the earlier chapel. It is built of large, stone boulders and is rectangular in shape, measuring 34ft x 15ft. Of simple construction, it has interesting features including a carved font and part of a cross socket at the east end which dates back to the 14th century. The front door is unusual because although it is rectangular for some unknown reason, it is set into a pointed doorway.

# St Justinian's Chapel –

## Porthstinian, Pembrokeshire

St Justinian's chapel is in a beautiful cove two miles west of St David's, overlooking the old lifeboat station and Ramsey Island.

St Justinian was a 6th century missionary. He came from Brittany and after being commanded by God to withdraw from the world, he set sail in a coracle to Ramsey Island, where he established a cell and lived as a hermit. He later became a friend, teacher and associate of St David's.

The chapel was built in the 14th century on the site of a much older shrine and was restored in the early 16th century by Bishop Vaughan. Although the existing building is now roofless, the overall stucture is still intact; however there is nothing remaining of the original artifacts or interior decoration.

There are many legends associated with St Justinian. One relates that St Justinian was murdered on Ramsey Island when his harsh regime became impossible to bear, his followers cut off his head. St Justinian then managed to swim to the mainland clutching his own head, and came ashore at St Justinian's Point, the spot where he wanted to be buried.

Through divine retribution, the murderers contracted leprosy and were banished to an outcrop off Ramsey Island known as Leper's Rock.

Another legend tells that in the 6th century, Ramsey Island was joined to the mainland by a narrow causeway of rock, leading to the saint being continuously interrupted from his devotions by numerous visitors. Unable to endure this any more, he prayed that the land-bridge be broken. His prayers were answered, and the rocks fell into the sea. All that remains of the causeway is a treacherous reef called the Bitches.

# St Dogmael's Abbey –

## Llandudoch/St Dogmaels, Ceredigion

The Abbey can be found in the village of Llandudoch on the Teifi estuary, opposite the town of Cardigan.

A religious settlement has been on this site for about 1400 years and an ancient carved stone pillar found in the church adjacent to the abbey suggests that there was a Celtic foundation dating back to the 6th century.

In the 7th century an early Welsh monastery was established here but was raided and destroyed by Vikings. The surviving abbey was built on the site of the Welsh monastery in 1115 by Sir Robert Fitz Martin. It was dedicated to St Dogmael who was a cousin of St David. The Benedictine monks who established the religious community here were originally from the French Abbey of Tiron, founded by St Bernard of Abbeyville. They led simple and austere lives in accordance to the rules of St Benedict.

Parts of the remaining building date back to the 12th century, with the west walls being added in the 13th century and the north transept being built in the Tudor period. This has traces of 16th-century vaulting with carved figures representing saints, such as a lion representing St Matthew, and an angel being the Archangel Michael.

Little remains of the monks' residential buildings; all that has survived is the monks' infirmary, and the chapter house footings.

The Abbey was closed during the dissolution of the monasteries; however, it was still used for a period as a parish church.

There is a legend associated with St Dogmaels which tells that during a storm off Cemaes Head, a mermaid saved a sailor named Penegrin and his fellow fishermen from drowning.

# St Beuno's Church – Clynnog Fawr, Gwynedd

This spectacular church dominates the village of Clynnog Fawr on the coast road in the north of the Llŷn Peninsula.

St Beuno is said to have been born on the banks of the River Severn in Powys, the son of noble parents, educated in Caerwent. He established a cell in Clynnog Fawr about 616 AD and was given land by King Cadwallon of Gwynedd on which he founded a monastery, which flourished until it was ransacked by the Vikings in the 10th century.

The present church is impressive in scale and architecture, especially when you consider its isolated position in this small village. It dates from the early 15th century, with the chancel and transept being built about 1480. The church was considerably enlarged just before the reformation, to accommodate the large number of pilgrims who gathered here to follow the 'pilgrims' way' to Bardsey Island.

Connected to the church is St Beuno's chapel – Eglwys y Bedd – which is only 15ft long, and is believed to be the shrine of St Beuno. When the chapel was restored in 1913, the foundations of a much earlier building were discovered beneath the floor; this may have been Beuno's original cell.

According to legend, when he died and before he was buried, there was a dispute between the religious communities of Bardsey and Nefyn who each wanted the saint's remains. They agreed to wait until the next day to solve the problem. During the night a miracle occurred, and in the morning, three identical coffins were found with identical contents, so everyone was happy!

Inside the church there is an unusual chest carved out of a solid wooden trunk. According to local tradition, farmers who had lambs or calves born with a notched ear (the mark of Beuno) would be sold and the money put into the chest, which was used to help the poor of the parish.

In the churchyard is an interesting feature, which is one of only two Celtic sundials in Britain. Nearby can be found St Beuno's well; the waters were supposed to be a cure for epilepsy and rickets, but a person could only be cured if they slept on St Beuno's Tomb overnight.

# Caldey Island Monastery –

## near Tenby, Pembrokeshire

Caldey Island is about 2 miles offshore from Tenby and is about 2 miles long by 1 mile wide.

There has been a long religious tradition on Caldey Island, with the first monastery established by St Dubricius in the 6th century, who appointed Pyr as the first abbot.

Unfortunately, Pyr met with an unholy death – when he was walking back to his cell one night, the drunken abbot fell into the monastery well and drowned.

St Samson replaced Pyr as the abbot in 521 AD. He endeavoured to stop the monks' intemperate behaviour and for a time the community became more peaceful, but after a few years the monks fell back into their old ways, so St Samson left the island and went to Stackpole, where he lived as a hermit in an isolated cave on the coast.

Caldey Island had an important religious community in the 6th century and in those days, a community of nuns was linked to the monastery on St Margaret's Island which adjoins Caldey.

The small parish church of St David's was built on the foundations of the original monastery, and inside can be found a stone, which is over 1,200 years old, inscribed with Ogham and Latin. In the 12th century Benedictine monks established a monastery here and remained for hundreds of years until the dissolution of the monasteries.

There are a number of buildings that still survive from this period, including the priory, refectory and gatehouse, which were built in the 12th and 15th centuries.

The Benedictines eventually returned to Caldey and built the present abbey; however, in 1929 this was taken over by the Cistercian monks who remain in residence today.

# St Winefride's Well and Chapel –

## Treffynnon/Holywell, Flintshire

St Winefride's Well and Chapel can be found in the town of Treffynnon which takes its name from the well.

St Winifride was born in the 6th century, the daughter of Prince Tefydd and Gwenth.

Legend tells that a Prince Caradog was in love with Winefride, but she rejected his amorous advances and fled from him. The prince pursued and caught Winefride and in a fit of rage cut off her head, which fell to the ground; at the spot where it landed, a fountain of water sprang up. Her uncle, St Beuno, who was preaching nearby, rushed to her aid and placed her head back onto her shoulders, restoring her to life. She lived the remaining 15 years of her life as a nun in a convent in Gwytherin near Conwy. When she died, her body was brought back to be buried in this shrine; however, in 1138 her remains were stolen and taken to Shrewsbury Abbey.

Pilgrims have been coming to St Winefride's Well for over 1,300 years and it is considered the greatest holy well in Britain; a number of kings have made pilgrimages here, including Edward I, Henry V and James II.

The chapel surrounding the well was built in 1483 by Lady Margaret Beaufort, the mother of Henry VII. It replaced a much earlier chapel which had become a crumbling ruin.

The present building has survived intact despite the reformation and civil war. It is a fine example of the perpendicular style of architecture. Inside the structure is a star-shaped well in the centre, and outside, a bathing pool was constructed which was used when there were large numbers of pilgrims visiting the shrine.

The well is supposed to have miraculous curative properties and is associated with curing women's ailments and skin complaints. Some of the stones in the well are covered with strange red markings which are said to be the blood of St Winefride.

# St Illtyd's Church –

## Llanilltyd Fawr, Glamorgan

This magnificent abbey-like church is dedicated to St Illtyd who helped to establish the monastery and college here in the 5th century. However, this site can claim to be the earliest seat of learning in United Kingdom, as a small college was established here early in the 3rd century by Eurgain, who was a daughter of Caractacus.

St Illtyd had come over from Brittany in France as a soldier of fortune and legends suggest that he was one of King Arthur's knights, named by some to be the original Sir Galahad, before he gave up his sword and became a monk.

St Illtyd was principal of the college, which combined Christian, classical, and druidic learning. It is thought that he was of druidic descent, having many of the powers associated with the druids.

The college became one of the most important centres of learning in Britain, where St Illtyd trained missionaries for work in Wales and France. Many well-known saints studied here, including St David, St Samson and St Teilo, but the college was destroyed by the Vikings in 987 AD.

The present building is unusual because it is two churches joined together. The old church, which is west of the tower, was the original structure, and this became the parish church. East of the tower is the monastic church, which was built in the 13th century.

There are a number of interesting features here, including a fascinating collection of Celtic stone crosses from about the 8th century. The church also has a stone rood screen dating back to the 14th century and a 1,000-year-old font. Attached to the church are the remains of the old monastery gateway.

# St Mary's Abbey – Ynys Enlli, Gwynedd

Ynys Enlli (Isle of Currents)/Bardsley Island is 2 miles off the tip of the Llŷn Peninsula. The island is about 2 miles long, dominated by a 550ft-high hill on the north eastern side, and is a wild and isolated place. This was a sacred site from very early times and Christians sought sanctuary here in the dark ages.

As early as the 3rd century, a church was founded here, and for centuries it was considered the holiest place in Wales, being an important place for Pilgrims to visit. In the middle ages, the island was considered such a holy site that three pilgrimages to Bardsey equalled one to Rome, and it was one of the most popular pilgrim routes in northern Europe.

The pilgrims would undertake a long arduous journey before finally arriving at St Mary's Chapel at Braich-y-pwll. All that remains of the chapel is a few pieces of masonry, and its outline in a grassy mound, situated above the shore from where they would have sailed across the treacherous Bardsey Sound to Enlli, their final destination.

Many pilgrims came to the island to die and it is reputed that 20,000 saints – including important saints such as St Padarn, St Deiniol and St Dyfrig – are buried here.

The first Celtic monastery was founded here in 516 AD by St Cadfan, who had come from Brittany in 429 AD. It was the last remaining bastion of the Celtic form of monasticism. Later, an Augustinian monastery dedicated to St Mary was built on the same site early in the 13th century, but only the tower and a few ancient stone crosses remain.

According to legend, Bardsey was also the home of Merlin the wizard, who is reputedly still there, guarding the 13 ancient treasures of Britain. At one time the island was called Ynys Afallon (Avalon) and may have been the place where King Arthur was taken to recover after he was severely wounded at the battle of Camlan.

# Margam Abbey – Margam, Glamorgan

There has been a Christian foundation here for over 1,000 years. A monastery was established by Celtic monks in the 9th century, but was destroyed by Robert the Consul, Earl of Gloucester, who gave the land to Cistercian monks from the French Abbey of Clairvaux.

So a new abbey was founded in 1147, taking forty years to build and becoming one of the largest and wealthiest in Wales.

Although the building has been renovated over the years, the abbey still retains some fine Norman features such as the arched doorway and the round-headed windows above.

A large number of early-Celtic carved monuments were discovered here. They can be found in the museum adjacent to the ancient church, housed in medieval buildings which may have been one of the oldest schools in Britain. Here are some of the finest stone crosses in Wales, including the great cross of Cynfelyn with its intricate knotwork carving.

The existing parish church was originally the monastic nave. Inside the building, the church is divided by large pillars into six areas, which also date to the Norman period.

Other features of interest inside the church are the tombs of the Mansel family and a stained glass window by William Morris.

Many legends are associated with Margam. They tell of awful deaths for anyone who offended against the laws of sanctuary or defiled the holiness of the abbey.

In addition, there are tales of miraculous events such as that which happened during a bad famine. A field of unripe wheat suddenly became ready for harvesting and the starving people were fed.

# St Hywel's Church –
## Llanhywel, Pembrokeshire

This church is on one of the old pilgrim routes to St David's and is dedicated to St Hywel.

He was the son of Emyr Llydaw and the brother of St Gwyndaf who were forced to flee from Brittany after a family feud. Legend claims that he was one of King Arthur's Knights, fighting with Arthur against Sir Lancelot, and helping in his wars with the Romans. When he died he was buried at Llanilltyd Fawr where he had studied.

There has been a religious settlement on this site since the 5th or 6th century, and the early church would have been connected with monastic foundations in the area. The first church would have been constructed of timber or drystone, being small in size. The dimensions of the existing church suggests its ancient origins.

The present building was built between 1115-1280 by Bishop Bernard of St David's, the nave and chapel being built in the 12th century and the vaulted chapel being built in the early 14th century. Features of interest include the remains of the lepers' window in the south west corner of the sacristy, and a fine leaded window in the north chapel which dates from the 15th century.

Outside the church, beneath the west window can be found a 6th century burial stone inscribed in Latin with the words 'Rinaci Nomena', which mean 'the remains of Rinacus lie here'. This stone proves that a Christian community was in this area at that time.

Following the pilgrims' road out of Llanhywel towards St David's, we find Dowrog Common, once known as the Pilgrims' Land where the medieval pilgrims could stay and rest after their long journeys. It was given to the church by Prince ap Tewdwr in 1080 for this purpose.

# St Gwyndaf's Church –

## Llanwnda, Pembrokeshire

The ancient church of St Gwyndaf can be found in a small isolated village overlooking Strumble Head, about two miles north of Fishguard.

Born in the 6th century, the son of Emyr Llydaw, who was a refugee from Brittany, St Gwyndaf became chaplain of Dyfrig's college in Caerleon about 540 AD. He founded Llanwnda church in the mid 6th century; when he retired, he went to Bardsey Island to die. There is a legend associated with the church which tells that St Gwyndaf had an argument with St Aiden in Fishguard, and as he was crossing the church stream upon his return, a fish leapt out of the water causing Gwyndaf's horse to rear, throwing the saint to the ground. He cursed the stream, 'that no fish would ever swim in it'. The spring still flows near the church, but since that day there have been no fish in the stream.

The existing church built on the old site is of a simple Welsh design, cruciform in shape with a double bellcote. Inside, the transepts widen into chantry chapels.

The church has six Celtic stone monuments built into the walls and there are four cross-marked stones dating from the 7th to the 9th centuries. One of the window sills has a stone, carved with the image of a cleric holding a staff. This may have been part of a broken stone cross.

A number of carved Celtic stones were found during the restoration in 1881. An interesting example in the east end of the south transept features a picture of a hooded woman.

In the porch can be found a leper's window, through which the lepers could see the altar and hear the mass.

There are a number of historical associations with this church. Asser, King Afred's biographer, was educated here and the famous Welshman Giraldus Cambrensis was rector here in the 13th century. Nearby is Carreg Wastad Point – it was here that over 1,400 French soldiers, under the command of the American Colonel Tate attempted an invasion of Britain in 1797.

# Capel Lligwy – near Llanalgo, Anglesey

This small chapel dating from the early 12th century can be found half a mile north of Llanalgo overlooking Lligwy Bay on Anglesey.

Capel Lligwy stands in an area which, during the period of the iron age settlements, must have been a centre of pagan worship. There are many remains of Neolithic monuments in this part of Anglesey; for example only a few hundred yards south of the chapel can be found Lligwy Burial Chamber. This is an impressive tomb with a large capstone weighing about 28 tons, supported by low stone pillars over a pit, where the remains of 30 Neolithic people were discovered during excavations in 1908.

The present chapel was built in 1125 and in the 14th century the building was altered, with additions being made to the walls. The chapel is of simple construction, being built of rough stones. Although it is now roofless, all four walls are standing to roof height, so it is easy to visualise how the chapel appeared in its heyday.

Inside the building, no decoration or artifacts remain, apart from a large ancient piscina carved out of a single rock. This probably dates back to the time the chapel was built.

The chapel now stands isolated in the middle of a field; it is a mystery why it was built in this location unless is was constructed on the foundations of an earlier chapel, in which case there could be a connection with the iron age village of Din Lligwy nearby. In this village are the remains of two round stone huts which date back to the late Roman period. 4th century coins and pottery found here suggest that it may have been occupied into the 5th century.

# St David's Cathedral – Pembrokeshire

St David's is the smallest city in Britain, and is one of the most important religious sites in the United Kingdom. Legends say that St David, patron saint of Wales, was born nearby in St Non's bay about the year 510 AD.

Descended from the old kings of Wales, he was the son of St Non, and was educated and took his vows as a monk at Whitland Abbey. From here, he travelled extensively as a missionary and is said to have founded 12 monasteries in Britain, including Glastonbury. When he returned to Pembrokeshire he spent the remainder of his life in this spot. He built a small monastery in St David's, half-hidden in a vale, which gave some protection against invaders; however, the church was raided many times by the Vikings in the 10th century.

The present cathedral dates from 1176. It was built following the canonisation of St David in 1120, and his shrine became an important pilgrimage centre – two journeys there equalling one to Rome.

The impressive building is cruciform in shape and was built by Peter de Leia and although the cathedral was damaged by an earthquake in 1248, the building has survived in good condition.

There are many superb architectural features throughout, especially inside the cathedral including the nave which is a fine example of 13th century craftsmanship. In addition, the 15th century woodcarving in the roof and choir stalls is very impresive.

The remains of St David are still kept in the cathedral in a cask situated in the north side of the presbytery, together with the relics of many other Celtic saints, including St Justinian.

# St Hywyn's Church –

## Aberdaron, Llŷn Peninsula, Gwynedd

To find St Hywyn's church, it is necessary to travel to the tip of the Llŷn Peninsula to Aberdaron, a picturesque village built around an old bridge. One building of interest is Y Gegin Fawr (The Great Kitchen), built as a resting place where pilgrims to Bardsey Island could shelter, rest, and buy food before their crossing over the hazardous Bardsey Sound.

St Hywyn's church is situated almost on the beach, with the lower half buried in the sand. The building overlooks an impressive curved beach enclosed by magnificent headlands.

It was originally founded in the 5th century by St Hywyn, a Celtic monk from Brittany. The present building dates back to the early 12th century. It was built on the site of Hywyn's first chapel, incorporating some of the original masonry.

Interesting architectural features include a Norman doorway and the two naves; the north nave is the oldest, with the south nave being added in the 15th century. This doubled the size of the church, to accommodate the large number of pilgrims who came to Aberdaron en route to Bardsey Island.

At the end of the north wall are two Celtic gravestones from the 5th or 6th centuries, which are believed to be the graves of two monks.

There are many stories associated with this location, including one which relates to a major political event at the church in 1115, when Gruffydd ap Rhys ap Tewdwr, king of Deheubarth, claimed the right of sanctuary inside the church when under threat from Henry I of England. He eventually managed to escape at night to the safety of his own kingdom.

# St Brynach's Church –

## Cwmyreglwys, Pembrokeshire

The ruins of this 12th century church are located on the Pembrokeshire coast in the village of Cwmyreglwys (Valley of the Church) at Dinas Head.

The original chapel was originally founded by St Brynach who came from Ireand. Most of his dedicated churches are found on coastal routes to Ireland, mainly in Pembrokeshire. He was thought to have been a forerunner of St Francis of Assisi because he had a magical way with animals and birds

Legends tell that he fled here, pursued by evil spirits, en route to Nevern where he settled. Another story says that the daughter of a ruling nobleman tried to seduce Brynach but he fled from her advances; she then sent soldiers to kill him, so he fled and escaped to Pembrokeshire.

All that remains of the church is the old bell tower and part of the west wall. However, the ruinous condition of the building is not due to years of neglect; it was actually destroyed in the great storm of October 1859 which ravaged this coastline, wrecking 114 ships, amongst them the Royal Charter.

Another storm in 1979 caused even more damage to the churchyard, leaving very little of the original building.

# St Cybi's Church –

## Caergybi/Holyhead, Anglesey

The church of St Cybi is in the centre of Caergybi overlooking the harbour. Its situation is quite unusual, as it was built in the centre of a 3rd century Roman fortress. The 16ft-high Roman walls are 6ft thick in places and surround the church, with towers at each corner. St Cybi obviously chose this site because of its protective situation. St Cybi established his church here in the 5th century with the existing church being built onto the remains of Cybi's original building.

St Cybi was a Celtic monk, probably from Cornwall, and after extensive travelling as a missionary, he eventually settled on Holy Island. He was buried in the south corner of the fort and a chapel was built over his grave.

The present building is mainly Tudor, although it was extensively restored in the 19th century by Gilbert Scott. Features of interest include superb 16th century medieval carvings in the porch, and stained glass windows by Edward Burne Jones and William Morris.

In the churchyard by the gate is the little church of Eglwys-y-Bedd (Church of the Grave), said to contain the tomb of Seregri Wyddel, the leader of a tribe of Irish raiders who held the fort in the 5th century. After many battles Seregri was killed by the Welsh chieftain Caswallon Llawhir ('Long Hand'). A few years later, Seregri was honoured by the Welsh, who admired his bravery and built the chapel to house his tomb.

# St Cwyfan's Church – Llangwyfan, Anglesey

St Cwyfan's church lies between two coves, Porth Cwyfan and Porth China in Llangwyfan Bay near Aberffraw on Anglesey.

The church was built on a very small circular island linked to the mainland by a 200-metre causeway, which is accessible only at low tide.

The church was first founded about 605 AD by St Cwyfan. Originally from Brittany, he was descended from Caradog Freich, and he founded religious communities in Llangwyfan in Denbighshire, Dyserth in Flint and on the Llŷn Peninsula.

The existing building was probably rebuilt in the late 11th century, with various alterations to the north side, such as the construction of a second aisle with an arcade. This, however, was removed after it was damaged by a storm about 200 years ago. The church was eventually restored in 1893.

Until the mid-nineteenth century, if bad weather or a high tide made the church inaccessible, services would be held in the local manor house, Plas Llangwyfan, which was nearby on the mainland. The priest would then claim a tithe consisting of two eggs, a loaf, a half pint of ale and hay for his horse.

This is probably one of the most spectacular locations in Wales, capturing the essence of the Celtic spirit and landscape.

# St Melangell's Church –

## Pennant Melangell, Powys

The church of St Melangell is located on the edge of the Berwyn mountains at the end of a narrow road in the Tanat valley near Llangynog. A church has been on this site for over 1200 years and some of the present building dates back to the 11th century. It is dedicated to St Melangell who lived in this valley. The legend suggests that she had fled from Ireland in the 7th century to avoid a forced marriage and after journeying great distances she eventually found refuge in Pennant where she lived for many years following the life of a hermit.

Folklore records that one day Prince Brochwel was hunting at Pennant with his hounds. While pursuing a hare, the prince encountered a young woman praying, with the hare hiding under the folds of her gown. The hounds were forced on by the hunter but then turned and fled, howling in terror. The huntsman raised his horn to his lips, but it made no sound and he was unable to remove it. The saint told the nobleman of her life and experiences. So impressed was the prince with her story that he gave her land in the valley, and here she founded a religious community.

Inside the church behind the main altar can be found the original 12th century shrine which is the earliest Romanesque shrine in Northern Europe. In the churchyard there are some very ancient yew trees which are over 1500 years old.

Over a number of years the church had been neglected, and by 1987 it was in such a bad state of repair that it needed major renovation, which was completed in 1992. During the restoration, archaeologists excavated the Cell-y-Bedd, and under the floorboards a cobbled stone floor and a stone slab were found. After further diggings, human bones were discovered, suggesting that this was an early Christian burial site, possibly containing the remains of St Melangell.

# St Non's Chapel & Well –

## near St David's, Pembrokeshire

There is little known about St Non, apart from the fact that she may have belonged to the family of Vortigern, a Celtic King. She was evidently of royal blood and became a nun at Tŷ Gwyn monastery at Maucan near Whitesand Bay which is a few miles from St David's. Legends tell that she was raped by Prince Sant and gave birth to St David. The birth was accompanied by thunder and lightning and the stone on which she was lying split apart by the force of the birth, leaving an impression of her hands upon it. Part of this stone was later used as an altar slab in her chapel.

St Non's chapel is located half a mile south of St David's, and can be found standing in the middle of a field in a beautiful location on the coast above St Non's Bay. The ruined building is possibly the oldest Christian foundation in Wales. Parts of the walls are still standing, and there is enough of the structure remaining to get a good impression of the original chapel. Inside the building, in one corner can be found a large white stone monument which has a cross inscribed in a circle, plus remains of stone coffins. Legend has it that this is the spot where St Non gave birth to St David, around 510 AD.

Near the chapel at the entrance to the field is St Non's well, which is covered by an arch roofed structure. The well reputedly sprang up during a thunderstorm at the very moment of St David's birth and its waters are said to cure infirmities – eye diseases in particular – and several miraculous cures are said to have taken place here. Many people visited the well during the middle ages.

St Non apparently died in western Brittany, and she has a fine tomb in Dirinon, France.

# St Patrick's Church – Llanbadrig, Anglesey

This church was founded in 440 AD and has a direct link to St Patrick, the patron saint of Ireland. St Patrick was born in Wales at Banwen, near Neath. At the age of 16, he was captured by Irish pirates who kept him in slavery for a number of years. When he eventually escaped, he returned to Wales to train as a priest, after which he was sent back to Ireland by Pope Celestine, to convert the Irish to Christianity.

A legend tells that when St Patrick was an old man, he met St Non and foretold that her child would become a great saint and prophet.

Another local legend suggests that during a bad storm, Patrick was shipwrecked on Ynys Badrig (Patrick's Island) and managed to scramble ashore. He eventually recovered in Patrick's Cave which has a freshwater well inside – Patrick's Well. This can be found just below the churchyard. After his recovery, St Patrick built a church to thank God for his survival.

The building is a simple construction of 60ft long by 14ft wide. The original chapel, however, would have been much smaller. This was enlarged by the Saxons in the 10th century and the site also became a cemetery. The bodies of Vikings and many early Christians were buried in and around the church.

One interesting artifact inside the church is a Celtic standing stone, decorated in the 7th century with carvings of a fish and tree. Outside, an unusual feature is a large stone archway at the entrance to the churchyard, said to be over 1000 years old.

# St Tanwg's Church – Llandanwg, Gwynedd

This ancient church was founded by St Tanwg about 450 AD. Little is known about the saint, apart from the fact that he was a Breton prince who escaped from Armorica and then studied at the Bangor of Ynys Enlli Monastery.

St Tanwg's church is one of the oldest Christian sites in Britain. For hundreds of years it was Harlech's mother church, and it was to be the base for St Patrick's mission. Out at sea, visible at low tide, is a deep ridge known as Sarn Badrig (Patrick's Causeway); legends suggest that it was a land link with Ireland, used by St Patrick as a crossing point.

For many years the building was also used as as a chapel of rest for corpses going to Bardsey Island for burial.

The church is situated at Llandanwg on the edge of the beach, surrounded by sand dunes which have to be cleared regularly to prevent it from being buried.

The oldest part of the church is the west end. It was originally very small, measuring approximately 35ft by 17ft inside, and it was illuminated by two little windows. The door in the south-west corner was replaced by the present doorway in the 17th century. In the 14th century the size was increased by about 25ft, with a large early-English window included in the east gable. The church contains two very early inscribed stones; the first, dating from the 5th century, is built into the east window of the chancel, and the other has Roman lettering from the 6th century, and is now in the south window of the chancel.

By the middle of the 19th century the church fell into neglect for many years, and the roof on the west end collapsed. The church filled with sand and was almost lost. However, due to public intervention, major restoration work was instigated and the church was rescued and re-roofed.

# The Hospice Church of St Beuno –

## Pistyll, Llŷn Peninsula, Gwynedd

This ancient church overlooking the sea can be found on the north coast of the Llŷn Peninsula. The original Celtic building was erected in the 7th century following the foundation of a monastery at nearby Clynnog Fawr by St Beuno, the most important of the North Wales saints and a descendant of the Princes of Powys. This was a hospice church used for worship by pilgrims en route to Bardsey Island. Pilgrims could rest in the adjoining hospice field and refresh themselves in the large pool next to the church after their long journeys. The first Celtic stone building was square in shape with a massive cornerstone, which would have been dragged for many miles to this spot, as it is not local stone. The rest of the church was then built onto this large boulder. In the early days there would have only been two windows, one being the lepers' window where lepers would stand to hear mass and receive the host. In the south of the building the original doorway and step, later replaced by the existing romanesque entrance, can still be seen. Inside the church, the font is of particular interest. It is of Celtic origin, with knotwork patterns depicting life without beginning or end.

In the churchyard, many ancient fruit bushes still grow, and old medicinal herbs flourish. In 1969 the local parishioners revived an archaic practice of strewing rushes and herbs on the floor of the church three times a year – at Christmas, Easter and Lammas festival in August. When entering the church, the rich aromatic smell can be inspiring and overpowering.

# Tintern Abbey – Tintern, Gwent

Tintern Abbey is one of the most impressive monasteries in Britain, situated on the banks of the River Wye, set against the wooded hills of the Wye Valley.

Tintern was built on the site of an earlier religious settlement established by St Tewdrig, King of Gwent, who had a cell here in 470 AD, and was eventually killed by the Saxons during a battle near this site. His remains were found during excavations in 1610, when his stone coffin was discovered beneath the north wall of the chancel.

The great abbey was founded in 1131 by Walter Fitz Richard, a Cistercian monk. The Cistertercians, known as the 'white monks' because they wore habits of undyed wool, insisted on such isolated places such as this spot to build their abbeys.

The Abbey church was consecrated in 1288, but had to be rebuilt in the 13th century, and later enlarged in the 14th century.

The church is very impressive, measuring 228ft long by 150ft wide with tall arches in the centre and a beautiful rose window in the east wall, which is 60ft above the high altar. A number of other monastic buildings attached to the abbey have survived, including the chapter house where the monks would meet each day to hear a chapter of their 'Rule', plus the refectory, kitchen and dormitories.

Tintern Abbey was closed in 1536 at the dissolution of the monasteries and gradually fell into decay; however the majority of the buildings remain in good condition.

Today it still retains its beauty, tranquillity and spiritual quality.

# St Brynach's Church & Cross –

## Nevern, Pembrokeshire

St Brynach's church is located in the beautiful Afon Nevern Valley, near the Pembrokeshire coast. The original chapel in Nevern was built by St Brynach as early as 540 AD. St Brynach was born in Ireland, and after travelling extensively, he settled in Pembrokeshire, becoming friends with St David. He was given land in Nevern by a local chieftain named Clether who had a hillfort on the peaks of Carn Ingli, which means 'place of angels', where St Brynach would converse with angels.

Little remains of the original chapel apart from numerous carved and engraved stones both inside and outside the church, including Vitialanus' stone which can be found near the porch and Maglocunus' stone which is set into the window sill in the nave. Both stones have bilingual inscriptions in Latin and 5th century Irish Ogham script.

In the churchyard is the great cross which is one of the finest examples of its kind in Wales. Almost 13 feet high, it was carved in the 10th century with intricate knotwork. There is an interesting tale associated with the cross; every year after the long harsh winters, the villagers of Nevern would wait for their harbinger of spring. On the 7th April (St Brynach's feast day) they would gather near the cross to await an extraordinary event: on that day each year, the first cuckoo of the year would arrive from Africa, landing on the cross and singing to announce that spring had arrived.

Another interesting feature of Nevern churchyard is the ancient yew trees which border the path leading up to the church. One of the twisted old trees has a dark red resin that drips from an old wound on the trunk. It looks very much like blood, and the tree is known as the bleeding yew. Some legends say that it bleeds for the sins of Wales; another story claims that a monk was hung from the branches for a crime that he did not commit. In his final moment, he proclaimed that the tree would bleed for ever, to confirm his innocence.

# Penmon Priory & St Seiriol's Church – Anglesey

On the far eastern tip of Anglesey, four miles from Beaumaris can be found the church of St Seiriol and Penmon Priory.

St Seiriol lived in the late 6th century on Anglesey and was the first principal of Penmon college. According to legend, he was buried on Puffin Island nearby.

The earliest churches on Anglesey were associated to the cells of hermits. Seiriol had a cell here and the remains can still be seen. Beside the cell are the 6th century foundations of his holy well, a small primitive building with seats and a square well, around which the local inhabitants would have gathered to pray. It was later enclosed by the existing 18th-century brick structure. The original church was built in the 7th century; however, in the 10th century there were many landings on Anglesey by the Vikings and the church at Penmon was raided and burnt in the year 971 AD. The church was eventually rebuilt in stone between 1120 and 1170.

Within the church are many interesting ancient artifacts and architectural features including the font which was originally the base of the 1,000-year-old celtic cross which can be seen in the south transept, plus a Saxon tower arch and arcading dating back to 1170.

Attached to the church are a number of monastic buildings including a three-storey 13th-century building which was the refrectory with cellars, dining room and dormitory.

Nearby is an impressive domed dovecot, built about 1600, which could house over 1000 birds.

# St Trillo's Chapel –

## Llandrillo-yn-Rhos, Gwynedd

This tiny stone chapel is located almost on the seashore at Llandrillo-yn-Rhos near Rhos on Sea.

The chapel was founded by St Trillo, a Celtic saint who lived in this area in the 6th century. He was the son of Hael of Llydaw and a brother of St Lleched and St Tegai. He was joined by St Mungo from Scotland to form a religious community on this site.

This area was an island until the middle ages, and would have been an ideal location to establish a settlement, as it was sheltered by surrounding forests. At low tide, it is possible to see the remains of medieval forests, and over the centuries some remains of these trees have been washed ashore.

This ancient structure was originally built in the 6th century, and is probably the smallest chapel in Britain, measuring only 11 feet by 8 feet. It was built, with thick walls of rough stone, over a holy well reputed to have healing powers for such ailments as rheumatism. In addition to this, it was also used for baptisms up to the 19th century.

Legends suggest that St Trillo built the chapel on this spot after seeing a vision of a Celtic cross of light appear above the sea here.

Near the chapel are the remains of a weir, which was originally constructed by Cisterian monk to catch fish and was still being used until 100 years ago. The fish caught here on every tenth day were claimed as a tithe by the local vicar of Llandrillo church.

Prince Madoc is said to have sailed to America from here in 1170 and discovered the continent 300 years before Columbus. A brass plaque in a nearby garden commemorates the historical voyage.

# St Govan's Chapel – Pembrokeshire

The chapel is located on the coast, about a mile from Bosherton in Pembrokeshire. This small chapel, only 20ft long and 12ft wide, is surrounded by the sea cliffs in a rocky crevice by the sea and parts of it may date from the 5th century. The present building is mainly 13th century and although now unused, is in reasonably good condition.

There are no artifacts and little decoration inside the chapel, but a tangible Celtic atmosphere can be experienced within its walls.

There are a number of legends associated with St Govan who is reputed to have been one of King Arthur's knights – Sir Gawain, who gave up his sword and became a monk after the quest for the Holy Grail.

According to one tale, St Govan hid in the ravine while being pursued by raiders; apparently the rocks closed over him, opening again only when the danger was over. Another story tells of the chapel's silver bell – which at one time hung in the now-empty bellcote – being stolen by pirates, who were shipwrecked by a sudden storm as they made their escape. The bell was then rescued by mermaids, who placed it on a nearby rock which rings when it is struck, giving off a note identical to that of the stolen bell. Tradition also claims that no-one is able to count the number of steps on the way down to the chapel and up again and arrive at the same total. Below the chapel is St Govan's well, which is now dry, but in the middle ages it was popular as the waters reputedly cured eye ailments.

# St Mary Magdalene – Bleddfa, Powys

Bleddfa lies in the north of Radnor Forest. St Mary Magdalene's church is situated in the valley, surrounded by hills. This is one of several churches in Wales to be dedicated to this saint. The building is essentially Norman, replacing an earlier Celtic structure. The earliest part of the present building is the narrow nave which dates from the early part of the 13th century, as suggested by the unaltered window of that date in the north wall. The building was later extended to double its original size at the end of the 13th century and the join between the old and newer walls can be seen clearly both on the inside and outside. This development was followed closely by the construction of a tower at the west end of the building which later collapsed in the middle ages, destroying part of the west end of the nave; the remains of which can be seen. The ancient beam above the entrance to the chancel suggests that there may have been a medieval screen, and the remains of the floral decoration may still be seen. Interesting features inside include a sandstone piscina set in the north wall of the chancel and an octagonal font stand at the west end; both date from the early medieval period. The ruins of an unusual structure with thick stone walls, almost the width of the church itself, can be seen at the back of the church. Its purpose remains a mystery.

# St Celynin's Church – Llangelynin, Gwynedd

St. Celynin was probably born in Ireland, however there are stories that he was one of the sons of Helyg ab Galanog who lived in a kingdom known as 'Cantref y Gwaelod'. The legends suggest that this was an enchanted land, rich and flourishing but following a major flood has since been submerged by the sea in Cardigan Bay. St. Celynin and some of the survivors escaped to Bardsley Island, becoming monks of St Cadfan's Cor and when he died was buried on the Island, which can be seen on the other side of the bay.

St. Celynin built his original cell on this site in the 6th century, which was constructed of stone and wood although nothing remains of this building. It is thought that at the end of the 7th or early 8th century the original cell was replaced by a more substantial chapel, there are some foundations and stonework dating from the 9th century which can still be seen. The existing church dates from the 11th and 12th century is built in an dramatic location on the steep headland overlooking the sea at Llangelynin. This simple building has thick walls, a plain, basic interior with little decoration however there are a number of interesting features, including a 15th century roof and a stone font that may date from the celtic period. In addition, the porch is very unusual as it is surmounted by a belfry.

In the churchyard can be found the grave of Abraham Wood, king of the Welsh gypsies – a family musicians who lived in this area of Wales during the 18th century. Abraham is buried close to the church door after collapsing on a road nearby.

# Llandaf Cathedral – Cardiff

In the west of Cardiff, about 2 miles from the city centre near the River Taf, can be found the cathedral of St Teilo. Built on a religious site dating back 1,400 years, the first church here was founded in the 6th century by St Teilo.

St Teilo was born near Penally in south Wales, the son of Enlleu and Gwenhaf. He trained as missionary at the college at Llanilltyd Fawr, after which he went to live in Brittany at St Samsons monastery in Dol for seven years; he planted vast apple orchards there. In Brittany he is still patron saint of apple trees and horses. After his stay in France he is reputed to have made a pilgrimage to Jerusalem with St David and St Padarn. Returning to Wales he established the monastery at Llandeilo Fawr, becoming an influential religious leader. St Teilo was one of the most popular of the Welsh saints, and soon after the cathedral was built, his remains were removed from Llandeilo and reintered at the new building to enhance its reputation. The cathedral was established by Bishop Urban. Building began in 1107 and continued for many years, incorporating a number of architectural styles.

There are a few features from this period remaining, such as the fine arch behind the high altar which is Norman in style.

In 1220 the west front was built and is one of the finest examples of medieval masonry in Wales. The chapter house was later added by Bishop Henry of Abergavenny and the northwest tower built in the perpendicular style of architecture by Jasper Tudor who was an uncle of Henry VII.

Over hundreds of years the cathedral fell into neglect and in the beginning of the 18th century there were a number of bad storms which severely damaged the building; one pinnacle fell to the ground in 1703 and a tower collapsed n 1723. In addition to this, during the civil war, Cromwell's soldiers used part of the church as an ale house; they also burned priceless books from its library. In 1941 the nave was destroyed by German bombs. In spite of all of these problems over the years the building has survived and is now fully restored.

For a full list of books currently in print,
send now for your free copy
of our new, full-colour Catalogue
– or simply surf into our website at
**www.ylolfa.com.**

Talybont Ceredigion Cymru/*Wales* SY24 5AP
*ffôn* 0044 (0)1970 832 304  *ffacs* 832 782  *isdn* 832 813
*e-bost* ylolfa@ylolfa.com  *y we* www.ylolfa.com